D1639475

Fopdoodle
and
Salmagundi

*Words and meanings from
Dr Johnson's dictionary
that time forgot*

Selected by
Edward Allhusen

·OLD·
HOUSE
BOOKS

ABBREVIATIONS:

adj. adjective; *adv.* adverb; *interj.* interjection; *n.* noun; *v.* verb.

Old House Books
Moretonhampstead, Devon, TQ13 8PA
01647 440707 info@OldHousebooks.co.uk

First published by Dr. Samuel Johnson in London in 1755 in his
Dictionary of The English Language.

The main entries are set in the Caslon typeface, the same that was used
in the original dictionary. William Caslon 1692–1766, a contemporary
of Samuel Johnson, created the typeface that bears his name in 1734
and it was used for many major publications in the eighteenth century.
It also crossed the Atlantic where it was used to typeset the American
Declaration of Independence in 1776.

This selection © Edward Allhusen, 2007
ISBN 978 1 873590 63 8
Printed in India

Old House Books publish reprints of books and maps that were
first produced a century or more ago. Our guide books and maps
are of interest to genealogists and local historians. Other titles have
been chosen to explore the character of life in years gone by and
are of interest to anyone who wishes to know a bit more about the
lives of their forebears.

For details of other titles published by Old House Books please visit
our website www.OldHouseBooks.co.uk or request a catalogue.

Samuel Johnson
1709–1784

When a group of booksellers commissioned an Oxford drop-out and struggling playwright to compile a dictionary in 1746 little can they have realised what an inspired choice they had made or that they had defined the greatest event in the history of the English language.

As a young man Samuel Johnson, the son of a Lichfield bookseller, had wormed his way through his father's books with unquenchable curiosity. At Pembroke College, Oxford his tutor described him as the most qualified student he had ever taught but a lack of funds forced him to leave before completing his degree.

When the booksellers approached him his estimate of three years for the completion of this new project, and his bold conviction to finish with little assistance, highlighted a somewhat misinformed optimism. Forty scholars at the Académie Française took over forty years to compile their dictionary.

Johnson, working with six copyists at his house in Gough Square (now a London museum), took nine years, still a remarkable achievement. First, Johnson would pore over innumerable texts from Milton and Shakespeare to scientific manuals and magazines, selecting passages to illustrate his definitions marking each and underlining the word to which the extract would be relevant. Later his assistants copied each extract onto a slip of paper. Only after three years, when this drudgery was completed for every letter in the alphabet and with every word appearing in any literature since the accession of Elizabeth I, did Johnson draft pages of definitions. As a book, it is almost autobiographical, often witty, at time ridiculous and always historically illuminating. It is perhaps the only dictionary that could be read from cover to cover to leave the reader stimulated as well as informed, especially if it is read with the intent of borrowing a few of the sadly forgotten words in this anthology and inserting them into every day vocabulary.

The booksellers paid an advance of £1575, roughly equivalent to £100,000 today, and all expenses were to be taken out of this sum, including the copyist wages for the whole nine years. The finished product contains over 2300 pages, 42,773 definitions, 114,000 illustrative quotations and, with a total word count of over 3,000,000, it is longer than the Bible. Each copy was priced at £4 10s, equivalent to £500 today. While it was not the earliest (a French dictionary was published in 1694 and the Italians had created one even earlier in 1612), its influence has been immeasurable with roles in Dickens and Thackeray's *Vanity Fair*. It was the standard dictionary for Wordsworth, Keats, Shelley, Austen, the Brontës, Trollope and Eliot. Perhaps if Shakespeare had lived to see it he would not have had to make up so much of his vocabulary.

Johnson was not rewarded with great fortune, but fame was assured and Oxford recognised his labours with an honorary doctorate. He died on 13 December 1784 and was buried in Westminster Abbey.

ABACTOR.

n. Those who drive away or steal cattle in herds, or great numbers at once, in distinction from those that steal only a sheep or two.

ABANNITION.

n. A banishment for one or two years, among the ancients, for manslaughter.

ABBEY-LUBBER.

n. A slothful loiterer in a religious house, under pretence of retirement and austerity.

ABECEDARIAN.

n. From a, b, c. He that teaches or learns the alphabet, or first rudiments of literature.

ABJECT.

n. A man without hope; a man whose miseries are irretrievable.

ABLIGURITION.

n. A prodigal spending on meat and drink.

ABORIGINIES.

n. Earliest inhabitants of a country; those of whom no original is to be traced; as the Welsh in Britain.

ABOVE-BOARD.

adj. In open sight; without artifice or trick. A figurative expression, borrowed from gamesters, who, when they put their hands under the table, are changing their cards.

ABOVE-GROUND.

adj. An expression used to signify that a man is alive, not in the grave.

ABRACADABRA.

n. Superstitious charm against agues.

Abscess.

n. A morbid cavity in the body; a tumour filled with matter; a term of surgery.

Absentee.

n. He that is absent from his station or employment or country. A word used commonly with regard to Irishmen living out of their country.

Absinthiated.

adj. Imbittered, impregnated with wormwood.

Accountant.

n. A computer, a man skilled or employed in accounts.

Accumb.

v. To lie at table, according to the ancient manner.

Acre.

n. A quantity of land containing in length forty perches and four in breadth or four thousand eight hundred and forty square yards.

Adder's-Grass.

n. A plant so named because serpents lurk about it.

Adder's-Wort.

n. A herb so named on account of its virtue, real or supposed, of curing the bite of serpents.

Addle.

adj. Originally applied to eggs and signifying such as produce nothing, but grow rotten under the hen; thence transferred to brains that produce nothing.

Addle-pated.

adj. Having addled brains.

Adipous.

n. Fat.

Adjutant.

n. A petty officer whose duty is to assist the major by distributing the pay and overseeing the punishment of the common man.

Adjutrix.

n. She who helps.

Admurmuration.

n. The act of murmuring or whispering to another.

Adread.

adv. In a state of fear, frightened, terrified.

Adulterine.

n. A child born of an adulteress.

Adultery.

n. The act of violating the bed of a married person.

Adventurer.

n. He that seeks occasions of hazard; he that puts himself in the hands of chance.

Afterclap.

n. Unexpected events happening after an affair is supposed to be at an end.

After-dinner.

n. The hour passing just after dinner which is generally allowed to indulgence and amusement.

Aftertossing.

n. The motion of the sea after a storm.

Agaze.

v. To strike with amazement; to stupefy with sudden terror.

Agrammatist.

n. An illiterate man.

Ague.

n. An intermitting fever with cold fits succeeded by hot. The cold fit is more particularly called the ague, the hot a fever.

Airling.

n. A young light, thoughtless, gay person.

Alackaday.

interj. A word noting sorrow and melancholy.

Alcohol.

n. An Arabic term used by chemists for a high rectified dephlegmated spirit of wine, or for any thing reduced into an impalpable powder.

Aleconner.

n. An officer of the city of London whose business is to inspect the measures of public houses. Four are chosen annually by the common-hall of the city and whatever might be their use formerly, their places are now regarded only as sinecures for decayed citizens.

ALEHOUSE.

n. A house where ale is publicly sold; a tippling-house. It is distinguished from a tavern where they sell wine.

ALGID.

adj. Cold; chill.

ALIFEROUS.

adj. Having wings.

ALTIOQUENCE.

n. High speech; pompous language.

AMARULENCE.

n. Bitterness.

AMATORCULIST.

n. A little insignificant lover; a pretender to affection.

AMAZON.

n. The Amazons were a race of women famous for valour who inhabited Caucasus; they are so called from their cutting off their breasts, to use their weapons better. A warlike woman; a virago.

Amorist.
n. An inamorato; a gallant; a man professing love.

Amper.
n. A tumour with inflammation; bile. A word said to be much used in Essex but perhaps not found in books.

Amygdalate.
adj. Made of almonds.

Anarch.
n. An author of confusion.

Anatiferous.
adj. Producing ducks.

Anileness.
n. The state of being an old woman.

Answer-jobber.
n. He that makes a trade of writing answers.

Antick.
adj. Odd; ridiculously wild; buffoon in gesticulation.

ANTIDYSENTERICK.
  adj. Good against the bloody flux.

ANTIPODES.
  n. Those people who, living on the other side of the globe, have their feet directly opposite to ours.

APRICATE.
  v. To bask in the sun.

ARIETATE.
  v. To butt like a ram.

ARITHMANCY.
  n. Foretelling future events by numbers.

ARMISONOUS.
  adj. Rustling with armour.

ARTERIOTOMY.
  n. The operation of letting blood from the artery; a practice much in use among the French.

ARTUATE.
  v. To tear limb from limb.

Ascii.

n. Those people who, at certain times of year, have no shadow on them at noon; such are the inhabitants of the torrid zone, because they have the sun twice a year vertical to them.

Asker.

n. A water newt.

Asperse.

v. To bespatter with censure or calumny.

Ass.

n. An animal of burden, remarkable for sluggishness, patience, hardiness, coarseness of food and long life.

Asshead.

n. One slow of comprehension; a blockhead.

Astrology.

n. The practice of foretelling things by the knowledge of the stars; an art now generally exploded, as without reason.

Atom.

n. Such a small particle as cannot be physically divided.

Auld.

adj. A word now obsolete, but still used in the Scotch dialect.

Auriferous.

adj. That which produces gold.

Australise.

v. To tend towards the south.

Awme.

n. A Dutch measure of capacity for liquids, containing eight steckans, or twenty verges or verteels; answering to what in England is called a tierce, or one sixth of a ton in France or one seventh of an English Ton.

Axillar.

adj. Belonging to the armpit.

B

BABBLEMENT.
n. Senseless prate.

BACCHANALIAN.
n. A riotous person; a drunkard.

BACKBITER.
n. A privy calumniator; a censurer of the absent.

BACK-FRIEND.
n. A friend backwards; that is an enemy in secret.

BADGER.
n. One that buys corn and victuals in one place and carries it unto another.

Badger-legged.

adj. Having legs of unequal length, as the badger is supposed to have.

Bagnio.

n. A house for bathing, sweating and otherwise cleansing the body.

Balbucinate.

v. To stammer in speaking.

Balderdash.

v. To mix or adulterate any liquor.

Baldrick.

n. A girdle.

Banstickle.

n. A small fish also called a stickleback.

Barbecue.

n. A hog dressed whole as in the West Indian manner.

Barber-Monger.

n. A word of reproach to signify a fop; a man decked out by his barber.

Barley Corn.

n. A grain of barley, the beginning of our measure of length; the third part of an inch.

Bastardy.

n. An unlawful state of birth, which disables the bastard, both according to the laws of God and man, from succeeding to an inheritance.

Batten.

v. To grow fat; to live in indulgence.

Battledoor.

n. An instrument with a handle and a flat blade, used in play to strike a ball, or shuttlecock.

Baubee.

n. A word used in Scotland and the northern counties for a halfpenny.

Bawd.

n. A procurer or procuress; one that introduces men and women to each other, for the promotion of debauchery.

Bawdy-house.

n. A house where traffick is made by wickedness and debauchery.

Beadroll.

n. A catalogue of those who are to be mentioned in prayers.

Beadsman.

n. A man employed in praying, generally in praying for another.

Beard.

v. To take or pluck by the beard, in contempt or anger.

Bear-Garden.

adj. A word used in familiar or low phrase for rude or turbulent; that is a man rude enough to be a proper frequenter of a bear-garden.

Beaver.

n. A hat of the best kind; so called from being made of the fur of a beaver.

Beavered.

adj. Covered with a beaver.

BECHICKS.
n. Medicines proper for relieving coughs.

BEDABBLE.
n. To wet; to besprinkle. It is generally applied to persons in a sense including inconvenience.

BEDLAMITE.
adj. An inhabitant of Bedlam; a madman.

BEDPRESSER.
n. A heavy lazy fellow.

BEDRAGGLE.
v. To soil the clothes by suffering them, in walking, to reach the dirt.

BEDRITE.
n. The privilege of the married bed.

BEDSTRAW.
n. The straw laid under a bed to make it soft.

BEDSWERVER.
n. One that is false to the bed; one that ranges or swerves from one bed to another.

Beer.

    n. Liquor made of malt and hops. It is distinguished from ale either by being older or smaller.

Begetter.

    n. He that procreates; the father.

Beldam.

    n. An old woman; generally a term of contempt, marking the last degree of old age, with all its faults and miseries.

Bellibone.

    n. A woman excelling both in beauty and goodness. A word now out of use.

Bellygod.

    n. A glutton; one who makes a god of his belly.

Belly-timber.

    n. Food; materials to support the belly.

Belswagger.

    n. A whoremaster.

Belweather.

    n. A sheep that leads the flock with a bell on his neck.

BEMONSTER.
v. To make monstrous.

BESMUT.
v. To blacken with smoke or soot.

BESPAWL.
v. To dawb with spittle.

BESPUTTER.
v. To sputter over something; to dawb anything by sputtering, or throwing out spittle upon it.

BETTY.
n. An instrument to break open doors.

BIBACIOUS.
adj. Much addicted to drinking.

BIBBER.
n. A tippler; a man that drinks often.

BICE.
n. The name of a colour used in printing. It is either green or blue.

BIDALE.

n. An invitation of friends to drink at a poor man's house and there to contribute charity.

BIESTINGS.

n. The first milk given by a cow after calving, which is very thick.

BIGSWOLN.

adj. Turgid; ready to burst.

BILBO.

n. A rapier; a sword.

BILBOES.

n. A sort of stocks, or wooden sheckles for the feet, used for punishing offenders at sea.

BILINGSGATE.

n. Ribaldry; foul language. A word borrowed from Billingsgate in London, a place where there is always a crowd of low people and frequent brawls and foul language.

BILK.

v. To cheat; to defraud, by running in debt, and avoiding payment.

BINARY.

adj. A method of computation in which, in lieu of the ten figures in common arithmetick, and the progression from ten to ten there are only two figures using the simple progression from two to two. This method appears to be the same with that used by Chinese four thousand years ago.

BIRDER.

n. A birdcatcher.

BIRDLIME.

n. A glutinous substance, which is spread on twigs by which the birds that light upon them are thus entangled.

BIRTHDOM.

n. Privilege of birth.

BISCUIT.

n. A kind of hard dry bread, made to be carried to sea; it is baked for long voyages four times.

BISHOP.

n. A mixture of wine, oranges and sugar.

BISSON.

adj. Blind.

BLAB.

n. A telltale; a thoughtless babbler; a treacherous betrayer of secrets.

BLACKBERRIED.

n. A little shrub that grows wild upon the mountains in Staffordshire, Devonshire and Yorkshire.

BLATANT.

adj. Bellowing as a calf.

BLATTERATION.

n. Noise; senseless roar.

BLEAKY.

adj. Bleak; cold; chill.

BLEB.

n. A blister.

Blench.
n. To hinder; to obstruct.

Blender.
n. The person who mingles.

Blinkard.
n. One that has bad eyes.
and
n. Something twinkling.

Blissom.
v. To caterwaul; to be lustful.

Blobber.
n. A word used in some counties for a bubble.

Blobberlip.
n. A thick lip.

Blockhead.
n. A stupid fellow; a dolt; a man without parts.

Blonket.
n. A blanket.

BLOODGUILTINESS.
n. Murder; the crime of shedding blood.

BLOODY-FLUX.
n. Cold, by retarding the motion of the blood and suppressing perspiration, produces giddiness, pains in the bowels, looseness.

BLOWZE.
n. A ruddy fat-faced wench.

BLUNDERBUSS.
n. A gun that is charged with many bullets so that, without any exact aim, there is a chance of hitting the mark.

BLUNDERHEAD.
n. A stupid fellow.

BLUNTWITTED.
adj. Dull; stupid. Ignoble in demeanour.

BOGGLER.
n. A doubter; a timorous man.

Boghouse.
n. A house of office.

Bog-trotter.
n. One that lives in a boggy country.

Bondmaid.
n. A woman slave.

Bonny-clabber.
n. A word used in some counties for sour butter-milk.

Booby.
n. A dull heavy, stupid fellow; a lubber.

Bookish.
adj. Given to books; acquainted only with books. It is generally used contemptuously.

Bootcatcher.
n. The person whose business at an inn is to pull off the boots of passengers.

Borrel.
n. A mean fellow.

BOTCHER.

n. A mender of old clothes; the same to a tailor as a cobbler to a shoemaker.

BOUNCER.

n. A boaster, a bully, an empty threatener.

BOUSY.

adj. Drunken.

BOUTISALE.

n. A sale at a cheap rate; as booty or plunder is commonly sold.

BRAGGADOCIO.

n. A puffing, swelling, boastful fellow.

BRAINPAN.

n. The skull containing the brains.

BRAINSICK.

adj. Diseased in the understanding; addleheaded; giddy; thoughtless.

BRANGLE.

v. To wrangle; to squabble.

BRAVO.
n. A man who murders for hire.

BREAKPROMISE.
n. One that makes a practice of breaking his promise.

BREEDBATE.
n. One that breeds quarrels; an incendiary.

BRONTOLOGY.
n. A dissertation upon thunder.

BRUNION.
n. A sort of fruit between a plum and a peach.

BUB.
n. Strong malt liquor.

BUBBLER.
n. A cheat.

BUBBY.
n. A woman's breast.

BUDGET.
n. A bag, such as may be easily carried.

Buffleheaded.

adj. A man with a large head like a buffalo; dull; stupid; foolish.

Buffoon.

n. A man whose profession is to make sport, by low jests and antick postures; a jackpudding.
and
n. A man that practices indecent raillery.

Bull-beggar.

n. Something terrible; something to fright children with.

Bumbailliff.

n. A bailiff of the meanest kind; one that is employed in arrests.

Bumpkinly.

adj. Having the manners or appearance of a clown; clownish.

Bungle.

n A botch; an awkwardness; an inaccuracy; a clumsy performance.

Burbot.
n. A fish full of prickles.

Bush.
v. To grow thick.

Bushy.
adj. Thick as a bush.

Butterfly.
n. A beautiful insect, so named because it first appears at the beginning of the season for butter.

Buxom.
adj. Obedient; obsequious, gay, lively, brisk.

Buzzer.
n. A secret whisperer.

By-coffeehouse.
n. A coffeehouse in an obscure place.

C

CABARET.

    n. A tavern.

CABBAGE.

    v. To steal cloth in cutting clothes.

CACHECTICAL.

    adj Having an ill habit of body; shewing an ill habit.

CACKEREL.

    n. A fish, said to make those who eat it laxative.

CALCULUS.

    n. The stone in the bladder.

CALKER.

n. A worker that stops the leaks of a ship.

CALLOW.

adj. Unfledged; naked; without feathers.

CAMELOPARD.

n. An Abyssinian animal, taller than an elephant, but not so thick. He is so named because he has a neck like a camel, he is spotted like a pard, but his spots are white upon a red ground. The Italians call him a giraffe.

CAMELOT.

n. A kind of stuff originally made by a mixture of silk and camel's hair; it is now made with wool and silk.

CAMISADO.

n. An attack made by soldiers in the dark; on which occasion they put their shirts outward to be seen by each other.

CANAL.

n. A bason of water in a garden.

Candlewaster.

n. That which consumes candles; a spendthrift.

Cankerbit.

adj. Bitten with an envenomed tooth.

Cannibally.

adv. In the manner of a cannibal.

Canter.

n. A term of reproach for hypocrites, who talk formally of religion, without obeying it.

Car.

n. A small carriage of burden, usually drawn by one horse or two.

Caravan.

n. A troop or body of merchants or pilgrims, as they travel in the east.

Cart-Jade.

n. A vile horse, fit only for the cart.

Cartoon.

n. A painting or drawing upon large paper.

CASEOUS.

adj. Resembling cheese; cheesy.

CASHEWNUT.

n. A tree.

CENSOR.

n. An officer of Rome who had the power of correcting manners.

CHIVALROUS.

adj. Relating to chivalry or errant knighthood; knightly, warlike; daring. A word now out of use.

CHOCOLATE-HOUSE.

n. A house where company is entertained with chocolate.

CHUET.

n. An old word, as it seems, for forced meat.

CHUFF.

n. A coarse, fat-headed, blunt clown.

CHUFFY.

adj. Blunt, surly; fat.

Chum.

n. A chamber fellow; a term used in universities.

Ciderist.

n. A maker of cider.

Cinder-Wench.

n. A woman whose trade is to rake in heaps of ashes for cinders.

Circumgyration.

n. The act of running round.

Cit.

n. An inhabitant of a city, in an ill sense. A pert low townsman. A pragmatical trader.

Clapperclaw.

v. To tonguebeat, to scold.

Clicker.

n. A low word for the servant of a salesman, who stands at the door to invite customers.

Clodpate.

n. A stupid fellow; a dolt; a thickskull.

Clogginess.
n. The state of being clogged.

Cloom.
n. To close or shut with glutinous or viscous matter.

Clown.
n. A rustick; a country fellow; a churl. A coarse ill-bred man.

Cluster-Grape.
n. A small black grape by some called the currant.

Cockatrice.
n. A serpent supposed to rise from a cock's egg.

Cockney.
n. A native of London, by way of contempt.

Cockshut.
n. The close of the evening, at which time poultry go to roost.

Coemption.
n. The act of buying up the whole quantity of anything.

COETERNALLY.

adv. In a state of equal eternity with another.

COFFEE.

n. A drink prepared from berries very familiar in Europe for these eighty years, and among Turks for one hundred and fifty. Brought into England by a Turkey merchant, in 1652. Coffee is a drink made of a berry as black as soot which they take, beaten into powder, in water, as hot as they can drink it. The drink comforteth the brain and heart, and helpeth digestion.

COFFEE-HOUSE.

n. A house of entertainment where coffee is sold and the guests are supplied with newspapers.

COGGER.

n. A flatterer, a wheedler.

COGGLESTONE.

n. A little stone; a small pebble.

COGNOMINATION.

n. A surname, the name of the family.

COLBERTINE.

 n. A kind of lace worn by women.

COLE.

 n. A general name for all sorts of cabbage.

COLLIQUEFACTION.

 n. The act of melting together; reduction to one mass by fluxion in the fire.

COLOQUINTEDA.

 n. The fruit of a plant of the same name, brought from the Levant, about the bigness of a large orange, and often called a bitter apple. Its colour is a sort of golden brown: its inside is full of kernels, which are to be taken out before it is used. Both the seed and pulp are intolerably bitter. It is a violent purgative, of considerable use in medicine.

COMEDY.

 n. A dramatic representation of the lighter faults of mankind.

COMING-IN.

 n. Revenue, income.

COMMODE.

n. The head-dress of women.

COMMONER.

n. One of the common people; a man of low rank; of mean condition.

COMMONS.

n. The vulgar; the lower people; those who inherit no honours.

COMPOTATION.

n. The act of drinking or tippling together.

COMPRINT.

v. The word properly signifies to print together; but it is commonly taken, in law, for the deceitful printing of another's copy or book, to the prejudice of the rightful proprietor.

COMPUTER.

n. Reckoner; accountant.

CONCUBINAGE.

n. The act of living with a woman not married.

CONDERS.

n. Such as stand upon high places near the sea-coast, at the time of the herring fishing, to make signs to the fishers which way the shoal of herrings passeth, which may better appear to such as stand upon some high cliff, by a kind of blue colour that the fish causeth in the water.

CONFABULATE.

v. To talk easily or carelessly together; to chat; to prattle.

CONFARREATION.

n. The solemnization of marriage by eating bread together.

CONGE.

v. To take leave.

CONSOPIATION.

n. The act of laying to sleep.

CONTRAVALLATION.

n. The fortification thrown up by the besiegers, round a city, to hinder the sallies of the garrison.

CONVENTICLER.
n. One that supports or frequents private and unlawful assemblies.

CONY.
n. A rabbit. An animal that burrows in the ground.

COOM.
n. Soot that gathers over an oven's mouth.

COPPER-NOSE.
n. A red nose.

COQUET.
v. To entertain with compliments and amorous tattle; to treat with an appearance of amorous tenderness.

CORNUTE.
v. To bestow horns; to cuckold.

CORROBORANT.
adj. Having power to give strength.

CORRUGANT.
adj. Having the power of contracting into wrinkles.

COSCINOMANCY.

n. The art of divination by means of a sieve. A very ancient practice mentioned by Theocritus, and still used in some parts of England, to find out persons unknown.

COSIER.

n. A botcher.

COTTAGE.

n. A hut, a mean habitation.

COTTAGER.

n. One that lives in a hut or cottage on the common without paying rent and without any land of his own.

COUNTERMARK.

v. A horse is said to be countermarked when his corner-teeth are artificially made hollow, a false mark being made in the hollow place, an imitation of the eye of a bean, to conceal the horse's age.

COUPLE-BEGGAR.

n. One that makes it his business to marry beggars to each other.

COVERT.

adj. The state of a woman sheltered by marriage under her husband.

COZENER.

n. A cheater; a defrauder.

CRACK-ROPE.

n. A fellow that deserves hanging.

CRICKET.

n. A sport, at which the contenders drive a ball with sticks in opposition to each other.

CRINIGEROUS.

adj. Hairy, overgrown with hair.

CROCITATION.

n. The croaking of frogs and ravens.

CROWDER.

n. A fiddler.

CUBATION.

n. The act of lying down.

CUCKINGSTOOL.

n. An engine invented for the punishment of scolds and unquiet women.

CUCKOLD.

n. One that is married to an adulteress; one whose wife is false to his bed.

CUCKOLDMAKER.

n. One that makes a practice of corrupting wives.

CUNNINGMAN.

n. A man who pretends to tell fortunes, or teach how to recover stolen goods.

CURFEW.

n. An evening-peal by which the conqueror willed, that everyman should rake up his fire and put out his light.

CURTAIN-LECTURE.

n. A reproof given by a wife to her husband in bed.

CUSTARD.

n. A kind of sweetmeat made by boiling eggs with milk and sugar 'till the whole thickens into a mass. It is a food much used in city feasts.

Cutpurse.

n. One who steals by the method of cutting purses; a common place practice when men wore their purses at their girdles, as was once the custom.

Cynanthropy.

n. A species of madness in which men have the qualities of dogs.

D

DALLIANCE.

n. Interchange of caresses; acts of fondness.

DAMNINGNESS.

n. Tendency to procure damnation.

DANDIPRAT.

n. A little fellow; an urchin: a word used sometimes
in fondness, sometimes in contempt.

DANGLER.

n. A man that hangs about women only to waste
time.

DAPATICAL.

adj. Sumptuous in cheer.

DEAD-DOING.

adj. Destructive; killing; mischievous; having the power to make dead.

DEAMBULATION.

n. The act of walking abroad.

DEARBOUGHT.

adj. Purchased at a high price.

DEATHWATCH.

n. An insect that makes a tinkling noise like that of a watch, and is superstitiously imagined to prognosticate death.

DEBARB.

v. To deprive of his beard.

DEBULLITION.

n. A bubbling or seething over.

DECEMBER.

n. The tenth month when the year began in March.

DECIMATION.

n. A selection by lot of every tenth soldier, in a general mutiny, for punishment.

Decollation.
n. The act of beheading.

Deemster.
n. A judge; a word yet in use in Jersey and The Isle of Man.

Deep-musing.
adj. Contemplative; lost in thought.

Deferents.
n. Certain vessels in the human body appointed for the conveyance of humours from one place to another.

Deflourer.
n. A ravisher; one that takes away virginity.

Deglutition.
n. The act or power of swallowing.

Dehorter.
n. A dissuader; an adviser to the contrary.

Delices.
n. Pleasures. This word is merely French.

DEMI-MAN.
n. Half a man. A term of reproach.

DEMONOCRACY.
n. The power of the devil.

DEOSCULATION.
n. The act of kissing.

DEPOPULATOR.
n. A dispeopler; a destroyer of mankind; a waster of inhabited countries.

DEPUCELATE.
v. To de-flower; to bereave of virginity.

DETERRATION.
n. Discovery of anything by the removal of the earth that hides it; the act of unburying.

DEUTEROGAMY.
n. A second marriage.

DEVILKIN.
n. A little devil.

Dewbesprent.
adj. Sprinkled with dew.

Didder.
n. To quake with cold; to shiver.

Disard.
n. A prattler; a boasting talker.

Discalceation.
n. The act of pulling off the shoes.

Discase.
v. To strip; to undress.

Dish-washer.
n. The name of a bird.

Dislimb.
v. To dilaniate; to tear limb from limb.

Displode.
v. To disperse with a loud noise.
and
v. To vent with violence.

DISWITTED.

adj. Deprived of the wits; mad; distracted.

DITHYRAMBICK.

n. A song in honour of Bacchus; in which anciently and now among the Italians, the distraction of ebriety is imitated. Any poem written with wildness and enthusiasm.

DIZZARD.

n. A blockhead; a fool.

DOGHOLE.

n. A vile hole; a mean habitation.

DOGSLEEP.

n. Pretended sleep.

DOGWEARY.

adj. As tired as a dog; excessively weary.

DOLLAR.

n. A Dutch and German coin of different value, from about two shillings and sixpence to four and sixpence.

DOLT.

n. A heavy stupid fellow; a blockhead; a thick skull; a loggerhead.

DOODLE.

n. A trifler; an idler.

DORR.

n. So named probably from the noise which he makes. A kind of flying insect, remarkable for flying with a loud noise.

DOSIFEROUS.

n. Having the property of bearing or bringing forth on the back. May be properly used of the American frog, which brings forth young from her back.

DOTARD.

n. A man whose age has impaired his intellects; a man in his second childhood; called in some provinces a twichild.

DOUBLE-DIE.

v. To die twice over.

DOWDY.

n. An awkward, ill-dressed, inelegant woman.

Downfallen.

adj. Ruined, fallen.

Downgyred.

adj. Let down in circular wrinkles.

Downsitting.

n. Rest, repose. The act of sitting down or going to rest.

Drab.

n. A whore; a strumpet.

Draffy.

adj. Worthless; dreggy.

Draggle.

v. To grow dirty by being drawn along the ground.

Dragon.

n. A kind of winged serpent, perhaps imaginary. Much celebrated in the romances of the middle age.

Dragoon.

n. A kind of soldier that serves indifferently either on foot or horseback.

DRIBLET.
n. A small sum; odd money in a sum.

DROIL.
v. To work sluggishly and slowly; to plod.

DRONISH.
adj. Idle; sluggish; dreaming; lazy; indolent.

DROUGHTINESS.
n. The state of wanting rain.

DRUDGER.
n. A mean labourer.

DULBRAINED.
adj. Stupid; doltish, foolish.

DUNCE.
n. A dullard; a dolt; a thickskul; a stupid indocile animal.

DYSPHONY.
n. A difficulty in speaking, occasioned by an ill disposition of the organs.

EAGLESTONE.

n. A stone said to be found at the entrance of the holes in which eagles nest, and affirmed to have a particular virtue in defending the eagle's nest from thunder. The stones of this kind, which are most valued are flat and blackish, and found, if shaken near the ear; a lesser stone being contained in the greater.

EAME.

n. Uncle; a word still used in the wilder parts of Staffordshire.

EARTHLING.

n. An inhabitant of the earth; a mortal; a poor frail creature.

EARWITNESS.

    n. One who attests or can attest anything as heard by himself.

EAVESDROP.

    v. To catch what comes from the eaves; in common phrase, to listen under windows.

EBRIETY.

    n. Intoxication by strong liquors.

ECLEGMA.

    n. A form of medicine made by the incorporation of oils with syrups, which is to be taken upon a liquorice stick.

ECONOMY.

    n. The management of a family; the government of a household.

ECSTASIED.

    adj. Ravished; filled with enthusiasm.

EFFEMINATE.

    v. To make womanish; to weaken; to emasculate; to unman.

Ejaculation.

n. A short prayer darted out occasionally, without solemn retirement.

Electricity.

n. A property of some bodies, whereby when rubbed so as to grow warm, they draw little bits of paper, or such like substances to them.

Elflock.

n. Knots of hair twisted by elves.

Ell.

n. A measure containing forty-five inches or a yard and a quarter.

Elumbated.

adj. Weakened in the loins.

Elysium.

n. The place assigned by the heathens to happy souls; any place exquisitely pleasant.

Emaculation.

n. The act of freeing anything from spots and foulness.

EMBOLISM.
n. Intercalation; insertion of days or years to produce regularity and equation of time.

EMBROTHEL.
v. To inclose in a brothel.

EMMET.
n. An ant; a pismire.

ENATATION.
n. The act of escape by swimming.

ENFOULDRED.
adj. Mixed with lightening.

ENGINEER.
n. One who manages engines; one who directs the artillery of an army.

ENIGMATIST.
n. One who deals in obscure and ambiguous matters; maker of riddles.

ENNEATICAL.
adj. Every ninth day of a sickness.

Envenom.
n. To tinge with poison; to impregnate with venom.

Enwomb.
v. To make pregnant.

Ephemera.
n. A fever that terminates in one day.

Epicure.
n. A follower of Epicurus; a man given wholly to luxury.

Epistler.
n. A scribbler of letters.

Epulation.
n. Banquet; feast.

Erenow.
adv. Before this time.

Erke.
adj. Idle; lazy; slothful.

Errhine.
n. Snuffed up the nose; occasioning sneezing.

ERUCTATION.
  n. The act of belching.

ESCARGATOIRE.
  n. A nursery of snails.

EUNUCHATE.
  v. To make an eunuch.

EUTHANASIA.
  n. An easy death.

EVAGATION.
  n. The act of wandering.

EVESDROPPER.
  n. Some mean fellow that skulks about a house in the night.

EVISCERATE.
  n. To embowl; to draw; to deprive of the entrails; to search within the entrails.

EXANIMATION.
  adj. Deprivation of life.

Excise.

n. A hateful tax levied upon commodities and adjudged not by the common judges of property, but by wretches hired by those to whom excise is paid.

Excubation.

n. The act of watching all night.

Excussion.

n. Seizure by law.

Exenterate.

v. To embowel; to deprive of the entrails.

Exhilaration.

n. The act of giving gaiety.

Exomphalos.

n. A navel rupture.

Exossated.

adj. Deprived of bones.

Exotic.

n. A foreign plant.

EXPILATION.

n. Robbery; the act of committing waste upon land by the loss of the heir.

EXSPUITION.

n. A discharge of saliva by spitting.

EYESERVANT.

n. A servant that works only while watched.

F

FABACEOUS.
    adj. Having the nature of a bean.

FABULOSITY
    n. Lyingness; fullness of stories; fabulous invention.

FACINOROUS.
    adj. Wicked; atrocious; detestably bad.

FACTORY.
    n. A house or district inhabited by traders in a distant country.

FADDLE.
    v. To trifle, to toy with the fingers, to play.

FAGEND.

n. The end of a web of cloth, generally made of coarser materials.

FAIN.

adj. Glad; merry; cheerful; fond. It is still retained in Scotland.

FAIRYSTONE.

n. It is found in gravelpits, being of an hemispherical figure; hath five double lines arising from the centre of its base, which meet at the pole.

FAITHED.

adj. Honest, sincere. A word not in use.

FALDSTOOL.

n. A kind of stool placed at the south side of the altar, at which the kings of England kneel at their coronation.

FAMBLE.

v. To hesitate in the speech.

FAMOSITY.

n. Renown, celebrity.

Fancymonger.

n. One who deals in tricks of imagination.

Fancysick.

adj. One whose imagination is unsound; one whose distemper is in his own mind.

Farm.

n. Land let to a tenant. Ground cultivated by another man upon condition of paying part of the profit to the owner.

Farthing.

n. The fourth of a penny; the smallest English coin.

Farthingale.

n. A hoop; circles of whalebone used to spread the petticoat to a wide circumference.

Fatkidneyed.

adj. Fat; by way of reproach or contempt.

Fatwitted.

adj. Heavy; dull; stupid.

FAUCHION.

n. A crooked sword.

FAUSSEN.

n. A sort of large eel.

FAXED.

adj. Hairy.

FEABERRY.

n. A gooseberry.

FEATHERDRIVER.

n. One who cleanses feathers by whisking them about.

FELLMONGER.

n. A dealer in hides.

FELO-DE-SE.

n. He that committeth felony by murdering himself.

FELONY.

n. A crime denounced capital by the law; an enormous crime.

Fensucked.

adj. Sucked out of marshes.

Feriation.

n. The act of keeping holiday; cessation from work.

Ferula.

n. An instrument of correction with which young scholars are beaten on the hand: so named because anciently the stalks of fennel (ferula) were used for this purpose.

Feuterer.

n. A dogkeeper; perhaps the cleaner of the kennel.

Fiddlefaddle.

adj. Trifling; giving trouble, or making a bustle about nothing.

Fig.

v. To insult with contemptuous motions of the fingers.

Figpecker.

v. A bird.

FIGURE-FLINGER.

n. A pretender to astrology and prediction.

FILCHER.

n. A thief; a petty robber.

FINDY.

adj. Plump; weighty; firm; solid.

FINGLEFANGLE.

n. A trifle.

FINICALNESS.

n. Superfluous nicety; foppery.

FIRECROSS.

n. A token in Scotland for the nation to take arms, the ends thereof burnt black, and in some parts smeared in blood. It is carried like lightening from one place to another. Upon refusal to send it forward, or to rise, the last person who has it shoots the other dead.

FIZGIG.

n. A kind of dart or harpoon with which seamen strike fish.

FLAGITIOUS.
   adj. Wicked; villainous; atrocious.

FLAMMIVOMOUS.
   adj. Vomiting out flame.

FLAPDRAGON.
   n. A play in which they catch raisins out of burning brandy and, extinguishing them by closing the mouth, eat them.

FLASHER.
   n. A man of more appearance of wit than reality.

FLESHMONGER.
   n. One who deals in flesh; a pimp.

FLESHQUAKE.
   n. Tremor of the body in imitation of earthquake.

FLEW.
   n. The large chaps of a deep-mouthed hound.

FLEXANIMOUS.
   adj. Having power to change the disposition of the mind.

FLIPP.

n. A liquor much used in ships, made by mixing beer with spirits and sugar.

FLITTERMOUSE.

n. The bat.

FLUSTER.

n. To make hot and dosy with drinking; to make half drunk.

FOG.

n. Aftergrass; grass which grows in autumn after hay is mown.

FOOTPAD.

n. A highwayman that robs on foot, not on horseback.

FOPDOODLE.

n. A fool; an insignificant wretch.

FOREDO.

v. To ruin; to destroy. Opposed to making happy.

FOREWORN.

adj. Worn out; wasted by time and use.

FORNICATOR.

n. One who has commerce with unmarried women.

FORTUNETELLER.

n. One who cheats common people by pretending to the knowledge of futurity.

FOULFACED.

adj. Having an ugly or hateful visage.

FOXHUNTER.

n. A man whose chief ambition is to show his bravery in hunting foxes. A term of reproach used of country gentlemen.

FRANTICKNESS.

n. Madness; fury of passion.

FREAM.

v. To growl or grunt as a boar.

FREEBOOTER.

n. A robber; a plunderer; a pillager.

FREN.

n. A worthless woman.

Frenchify.
v. To infect with the manner of France.

Friarlike.
adv. Monastick; unskilled in the world.

Fribbler.
n. A trifler.

Fripperer.
n. One who deals in old things vamped up.

Frisk.
n. A frolick; a fit of wanton gaiety.

Frorne.
adj. Frozen; congealed with cold.

Frump.
v. To mock; to browbeat.

Frush.
v. To break, bruise, or crush.

Fub.
n. A plump chubby boy.

FUDDLE.
    v. To drink to excess.

FUGH.
    interj. An expression of abhorrence.

FULGID.
    adj. Shining; glittering; dazzling.

FULHAM.
    n. False dice.

FULIMART.
    n. A kind of stinking ferret.

FULL-BOTTOMED.
    adj. Having a large bottom.

FUMETTE.
    n. A word introduced from the French by cooks and the pupils of cooks, for the stink of meat.

FURACIOUS.
    adj. Thievish; inclined to steal.

FUST.
    v. To grow mouldy; to smell ill.

FUSTIAN.

n. Low fellow; a stinkard; a scoundrel.

FUTILE.

adj. Talkative; loquacious.

FUTTOCKS.

n. The lower timbers that hold the ship together.

FY.

interj. A word of blame and disapprobation.

G

GAD.
   v. To ramble about without any settled purpose; to rove loosely and idly.

GAFFER.
   n. A word of respect now obsolete, or applied only in contempt to a mean person.

GALERICULATE.
   adj. Covered as with a hat.

GALLANT.
   n. A gay, sprightly airy, splendid man.
   and
   n. A whoremaster who caresses women to debauch them.

GALLIGASKINS.

n. Large open hose.

GALLIMAUFRY.

n. A hoch-poch or hash of several sorts of broken meat.

GALLOW.

v. To terrify; to fright.

GAMBLER.

n. A knave whose practice it is to invite the unwary to game and cheat them.

GAMESOMELY.

adv. Merrily.

GANCH.

v. To drop from a high place upon hooks by way of punishment, a practice in Turkey.

GANTELOPE.

n. A military punishment in which the criminal running between the ranks receives a lash from each man.

Garbage.
n. The bowels; the offal; that part of the inwards which is separated and thrown away.

Gargarise.
v. To wash the mouth with medicated liquors.

Garlick.
n. Bulbous root with an extremely strong, and to most people, a disagreeable smell, and of an acrid and pungent taste. It is an extremely active and penetrating medicine, as may be proved by applying plaisters of garlick to the soles of the feet, which will in a very little time give a strong smell to the breath.

Garlickeater.
n. A mean fellow.

Gas.
n. A word invented by the chemists which seems to signify a spirit not capable of being coagulated.

Gay.
adj. Airy; cheerful; merry; frolick.

GAZEHOUND.
   n. A hound that pursues not by the scent but by the eye.

GAZINGSTOCK.
   n. A person gazed at with scorn or abhorrence.

GEASON.
   adj. Wonderful.

GEE.
   v. A term used by waggoners to their horses when they would have them go faster.

GELID.
   adj. Extremely cold.

GEMELLIPAROUS.
   adj. Bearing twins.

GEMMOSITY.
   n. The quality of being a jewel.

GENTRY.
   n. Class of people above the vulgar; those between the vulgar and the nobility.

GEOMANCER.

n. A fortuneteller; a caster of figures; a cheat who pretends to foretell futurity by other means than the astrologer.

GERMAN.

adj. Related.

GEWGAW.

n. A showy trifle, a toy; a bauble; a splendid plaything.

GIBCAT.

n. An old worn-out cat.

GIDDYBRAINED.

adj. Careless; thoughtless.

GIGGLE.

v. To laugh idly; to titter; to grin with merry levity. It is retained in Scotland.

GIGLET.

n. A wanton; a lascivious girl.

GINGERNESS.

n. Niceness; tenderness.

GIP.
v. To take out the guts of herrings.

GLABRITY.
n. Smoothness; baldness.

GLAIRE.
v. To smear with the white of an egg.

GLASSGAZING.
adj. Often contemplating himself in a mirror.

GLEEK.
n. Music; or musician.

GLIKE.
n. A sneer; a scoff; a flout.

GLOAT.
v. To cast side glances as a timorous lover.

GLOSSARY.
n. A dictionary of obscure or antiquated words.

GLOUT.
v. To pout; to look sullen. It is still used in Scotland.

GLOZE.

v. To flatter, to wheedle, to insinuate; to fawn.

GNOMONICKS.

n. To find the just proportions of shadows for the construction of all kinds of sun and moon dials and for knowing what o'clock it is.

GO-CART.

n. A machine in which children are enclosed to teach them to walk, and which they push forward without danger of falling.

GORBELLY.

n. A big paunch; a swelling belly. A term of reproach for a fat man.

GOSSIP.

n. One who answers for the child in baptism.
and
n. A tippling companion.

GRABBLE.

v. To grope; to feel eagerly with the hands.

GRAVY.

n. The serous juice that runs from flesh not much dried by the fire.

GRAY.

n. A badger.

GRAYBEARD.

n. An old man, in contempt.

GREATBELLIED.

adj. Pregnant; teeming.

GREAVES.

n. Armour for the legs; a sort of boots.

GREECE.

n. A flight of steps.

GREGAL.

adj. Belonging to a flock.

GREMIAL.

adj. Pertaining to the lap.

GRICE.

n. A little pig.

GRIMALKIN.

n. Grey little woman; the name of an old cat.

GRIPLE.

n. A greedy snatcher, a griping miser.

GRISKIN.

n. The vertebrae of hog boiled.

GROAT.

n. A piece valued at four pence.

GROPE.

v. To feel where one cannot see.

GRUBBLE.

n. To feel in the dark.

GRUBSTEET.

n. Originally the name of a street in Moorfields in London, much inhabited by writers of small histories, dictionaries and poems.

GRUM.

adj. Sour; surly; severe.

GRUMLEY.

adv. Sullenly, morosely.

GRY.

n. Anything of little value; as the pairing of the nails.

GUGGLE.

v. To sound as water running with intermissions out of a narrow mouthed vessels.

GUINEA.

n. A gold coin valued at one and twenty shillings.

GULCHIN.

n. A little glutton.

GULL.

n. A cheat; a fraud; a trick.

GUTTLE.

v. To feed luxuriously, to gormandise.

GYNECOCRASAY.

n. Petticoat government, female power.

Habnab.

adv. At random; at the mercy of chance; without any rule or certainty of effect.

Hackney.

n. A hireling, a prostitute.

Haft.

n. A handle; that part of any instrument that is taken into the hand.

Halcyon.

n. A bird, of which it is said that she breeds in the sea, and that there is always a calm during her incubation.

Half-scholar.
n. Imperfectly learned.

Hallucination.
n. Error; blunder; mistake; folly.

Halm.
n. Straw.

Hamated.
adj. Hooked; set with hooks.

Hanaper.
n. A treasury; an exchequer. The clerk of the hanaper receives the fees due to the king for the seal of charters and patents.

Harlequin.
n. A buffoon who plays tricks to divert the populace.

Harridan.
n. A decayed strumpet.

Hastings.
n. Peas that come early.

Hatchet-face.

n. An ugly face; such, I suppose, as might be hewn out of a block by a hatchet.

Havock.

interj. A word of encouragement to slaughter.

Haw.

v. To speak slowly with frequent intermission and hesitation.

Headborough.

n. A constable; a subordinate constable.

Heart-breaker.

n. A woman's curls, supposed to break the heart of all her lovers.

Heaven-begot.

adj. Begot by a celestial power.

Hebdomad.

n. A week; a space of seven days.

Hecatomb.

n. A sacrifice of an hundred cattle.

Hector.

n. A bully; a blustering, turbulent, pervicacious, noisy fellow.

Hedge-born.

adj. Of no known birth; meanly born.

Hedge-pig.

n. A young hedge-hog.

Hell-bred.

adj. Produced in hell.

Hell-broth.

n. A composition boiled up for infernal purposes.

Hell-governed.

adj. Directed by hell.

Helminthick.

adj. Relating to worms.

Hemicrany.

n. A pain that affects only one part of the brain at a time.

Hexapod.

n. An animal with six feet.

Higgler.

n. One who sells provisions by retail.

High-flier.

n. One that carries his opinions to extravagance.

High-viced.

adj. Enormously wicked.

Hindberries.

n. The same as raspberries.

Hobit.

n. A small mortar to shoot little bombs.

Hoiden.

n. An ill-taught awkward country girl.
and
v. To romp indecently.

Holderforth.

n. An haranguer; one who speaks in publick.

HOLOGRAPH.

n. This word is used in the Scottish law to denote a deed written altogether by the granter's own hand.

HONEY-MOON.

n. The first month after marriage, when there is nothing but tenderness and pleasure.

HOOK.

n. A field sown two years running.

HOROMETRY.

n. The act of measuring hours.

HOT.

adj. Lustful; lewd.

HOTCOCKLES.

n. A play in which one covers his eyes and guesses who strikes him.

HUGGERMUGGER.

n. A hug in the dark.

HUMBLEBEE.

n. A buzzing wild bee.

Humicubation.

n. The act of lying on the ground.

Humorous.

adj. Full of grotesque or odd images.

Hunks.

n. A covetous sordid wretch; a miser; a curmudgeon.

Hussy.

n. A sorry or bad woman; a worthless wench. It is often used ludicrously in slight disapprobation.

Huswife.

v. A bad manager; a sorry woman.

Hystericks.

n. Fits of women, supposed to proceed from disorders in the womb.

I

Iatroleptick.
adj. That which cures by anointing.

Icehouse.
n. A house in which ice is reposited against the warm months.

Ignivomous.
adj. Vomiting fire.

Ignoble.
adj. Mean of birth; not noble; not of illustrious race; worthless; not deserving honour.

Illachrymable.
adj. Incapable of weeping.

ILLNATURE.
n. Habitual malevolence.

IMBOSOM.
v. To admit to the heart, or to affection.

IMPENNOUS.
adj. Wanting wings.

IMPIGNORATE.
v. To pawn; to pledge.

IMPLORER.
n. Solicitor.

INCEPTOR.
n. A beginner; one who is in his rudiments.

INCH.
n. A measure of length supposed equal to three grains of barley laid end to end; the twelfth part of a foot.

INCOG.
adv. Unknown; in private.

INCONTINENT.
adj. Unchaste; indulging unlawful pleasure.

INFANGTHEF.

n. A privilege or liberty granted unto lords of certain manors to judge any thief taken within their fee.

INFAUSTING.

n. The act of making unlucky.

INGANNATION.

n. Cheat; fraud; deception; juggle; delusion; imposture; trick; flight.

INGATHERING.

n. The act of getting in the harvest.

INNINGS.

n. Lands recovered from the sea.

INSECTATOR.

n. One that persecutes or harasses with pursuit.

INSPECTOR.

n. A prying examiner.

INSPISSATE.

v. To thicken; to make thick.

INSUSURRATION.
  n. The act of whispering.

INTERCOMMON.
  v. To feed at the same table.

INTERMARRIAGE.
  n. Marriage between two families, where each takes one and gives another.

INTERWISH.
  v. To wish mutually to each other.

INTONATION.
  n. The act of thundering.

INURN.
  v. To intomb; to bury.

IRRADIATION.
  n. The act of emitting beams of light.

IRRISION.
  n. The act of laughing at another.

J

JACKALENT.
n. A simple sheepish fellow.

JACKPUDDING.
n. A zani; a merry-andrew.

JADE.
n. A horse of no spirit; a hired horse; a worthless nag.
and
n. A sorry woman. A word of contempt noting sometimes age, but generally vice.

JANGLE.
v. To altercate, to quarrel; to bicker in words.

JANGLER.
n. A wrangling, chattering, noisy fellow.

JANNOCK.

n. Oatbread. A northern word.

JEGGET.

n. A kind of sausage.

JET.

n. A very beautiful fossil of a firm and very even structure and of a smooth surface; seldom of a great size. The ancients recommended jet in medicine but it is now used only in toys.

JETTY.

adj. Made of jet; black as a jet.

JIGGUMBOB.

n. A trinket; a knick-knack; a slight contrivance in machinery.

JOBBERNOWL.

n. Loggerhead, blockhead.

JOCOSE.

adj. Merry; waggish; given to jest.

JOCUNDLY.

adv. Merrily; gaily.

Jogger.

  n. One who moves heavily and dully.

Jowler.

  n. A kind of hunting dog or beagle.

Jumble.

  n. Confused mixture; violent and confused agitation.

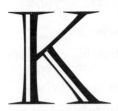

KECK.

v. To heave the stomach; to reach at vomiting.

KELL.

n. A sort of pottage. It is so called in Scotland, being a soup made with shredded greens.

KENNEL.

v. To lie; to dwell; used of beasts and of man in contempt.

KICKSHAW.

n. Something uncommon; something ridiculous. *and*
n. A dish so changed by the cookery that it can scarcely be known.

Kicksy-wicksey.

n. A made word in ridicule and disdain of a wife.

Kingsevil.

n. A scrofulous distemper, in which the glands are ulcerated, commonly believed to be cured by the touch of the king.

Kissingcrust.

n. Crust formed when one loaf in the oven touches another.

Kitchenwench.

n. Scullion; maid employed to clean the instruments of cookery.

Knacker.

n. A maker of small work.

Knapple.

v. To break off with a sharp quick noise.

Kneed.

adj. Having knees.

Knubble.

   v. To beat.

Knuckle.

   v. To submit. The custom of striking the under side of the table with the knuckles, in confession of an argumental defeat.

Knuff.

   n. A lout.

L

LABIAL.
   adj. Uttered by the lips.

LACED MUTTON.
   n. An old word for a whore.

LACHRYMATORY.
   n. A vessel in which tears are gathered to honour the dead.

LACKBRAIN.
   n. One that wants wit.

LACKLINEN.
   adj. Wanting shirts.

LADY.

   n. A woman of high rank; the title of lady properly belongs to the wives of knights, of all degrees above them, and to the daughters of earls, and all of higher ranks.

LAMBS-WOOL.

   n. Ale mixed with pulp of roasted apples.

LAMM.

   v. To beat soundly with a cudgel.

LANDJOBBER.

   n. One who buys and sells land for other men.

LANDLOPER.

   n. A landman; a term of reproach used by seamen of those who pass their lives on shore.

LAPIDATE.

   v. To kill by stoning.

LARGITION.

   n. The act of giving.

Lass.

n. A girl; a maid; a young woman; used only of mean girls.

Lasslorn.

n. Forsaken by his mistress.

Latish.

adj. Somewhat late.

Latitation.

n. The state of lying concealed.

Latitudinarian.

n. One who departs from orthodoxy.

Latrant.

adj. Barking.

Laudanum.

n. A soporifick tincture.

Lavatory.

n. A wash; something in which parts diseased are washed.

Lawn.

   n. An open space between woods.

Laystall.

   n. An heap of dung.

Lazar.

   n. One deformed and nauseous with filthy and pestilential diseases.

Lazar-house.

   n. A house for the reception of the diseased; an hospital.

Lecher.

   n. A whoremaster.

Leech.

   n. A physician; a professor of the art of healing.

Legerdemain.

   n. Slight of hand; juggle; power of deceiving the eye by nimble motion; trick; deception; knack.

Leman.

   n. A sweetheart, a gallant or a mistress.

Lethe.

   n. Oblivion; a draught of oblivion.

Levet.

   n. A blast on the trumpet; probably that by which the soldiers are called in the morning.

Lewdster.

   n. A lecher, one given to criminal pleasures.

Lexicographer.

   n. A writer of dictionaries; a harmless drudge, that busies himself in tracing the original, and detailing the significance of words.

Libation.

   n. The act of pouring wine on the ground in honour of some deity.

Libertine.

   adj. Licentious; irreligious.

Librarian.

   n. One who transcribes or copies books.

Licentiousness.

n. Boundless liberty; contempt of just restraint.

Lickerishness.

n. Niceness of palate.

Lifeweary.

adj. Wretched; tired of living.

Lig.

v. To lie.

Lightfingered.

adj. Nimble at conveyance; thievish.

Liking.

adj. Plump; in a state of plumpness.

Limbo.

n. A region bordering upon hell, in which there is neither pleasure nor pain. Popularly hell.

Limmer.

n. A mongrel.

LINKBOY.

n. A boy that carries a torch to accommodate passengers with light.

LINSTOCK.

n. A staff of wood with a match at the end of it, used by gunners in firing cannon.

LION.

n. The fiercest and most magnanimous of four footed beasts.

LIPLABOUR.

n. Action of the lips without concurrence of the mind; words without sentiments.

LIPWISDOM.

n. Wisdom in talk without practice.

LITHOMANCY.

n. Prediction by stones.

LIVERGROWN.

adj. Having a great liver.

LOB'S POUND.

n. A prison probably for idlers, or sturdy beggars.

Locomotive.
adj. Changing place; having the power of removing or changing place.

Loggerhead.
n. A dolt, a blockhead; a thickscull.

Longimanous.
adj. Long-handed, having long hands.

Loo.
n. A game of cards.

Loom.
v. To appear at sea.

Loover.
n. An opening for the smoke to go out in the roof of a cottage.

Losel.
n. A scoundrel; a sorry worthless fellow.

Lousy.
adj. Swarming with lice.
and
adj. Mean; low born; bred on the dunghill.

LOVETHOUGHT.
n. Amorous fancy.

LOVETOY.
n. Small presents given by lovers.

LOWBELL.
n. A kind of fowling in the night, in which the birds are wakened by a bell and lured by a flame into a net.

LUBBARD.
n. A lazy sturdy fellow.

LUCRE.
n. Gain; profit; pecuniary advantage. In an ill sense.

LURKER.
n. A thief that lies in wait.

LUXURIOUS.
adj. Delighting in the pleasures of the table.

LYCANTHROPY.
n. A kind of madness in which men have the qualities of wild beasts.

MACAROON.
n. A coarse, rude, low fellow.

MACILENT.
adj. Lean.

MACTATION.
n. The act of killing for sacrifice.

MAD.
n. An earth worm.

MADCAP.
n. A madman; a wild hot brained fellow.

MADGEHOWLET.
n. An owl.

Maffle.
v. To stammer.

Maggottiness.
n. The state of abounding with maggots.

Maidenhead.
n. Virginity; virgin purity; freedom from contamination.

Maidmarian.
n. A kind of dance, so called from a buffoon dressed like a man, who plays tricks to the populace.

Makebate.
n. Breeder of quarrels.

Malapert.
adj. Saucy; quick with impudence; sprightly without respect or decency.

Man.
n. Not a woman.

Mangler.
n. A hacker; one that destroys bunglingly.

MANUMIT.

v. To release from slavery.

MANURE.

v. To cultivate by manual labour.

MARMALADE.

n. The pulp of quinces boiled into a consistence with sugar: it is subastringent and grateful to the stomach.

MARRIAGEABLE.

adj. Fit for wedlock.

MAUNDER.

v. To grumble; to murmur.

MAZY.

v. Perplexed; confused.

MEACOCK.

n. An uxorious or effeminate man.

MECHANICK.

n. A manufacturer; a low workman.

MEDIC.

n. A plant.

MEDITERRANEAN.

adj. Encircled with land.

MELLIFLUENT.

adj. Flowing with honey; flowing with sweetness.

MERCURIFICATION.

adj. The act of mixing anything with quicksilver.

MERETICIOUS.

adj. Whorish; such as is practiced by prostitutes; alluring by false show.

MERRY-ANDREW.

n. A buffoon; a zany; a jack-pudding.

MERRYTHOUGHT.

n. A forked bone on the body of fowls; so called because boys and girls pull in play at the two sides, the longest part broken off betokening priority of marriage.

METEOR.

n. Any bodies in the air or sky that are of a flux and transitory nature.

METEOROLOGIST.

n. A man skilled in meteors or studious of them.

MEWL.

v. To squall as a child.

MIASM.

n. Such particles or atoms as are supposed to arise from distempered, putrefying, or poisonous bodies and to affect people at a distance.

MICHER.

n. A lazy loiterer, who skulks about in corners and by-places, and keeps out of sight; a hedge creeper.

MICKLE.

adj. Much; great. In Scotland it is pronounced Muckle.

MIDNIGHT.

n. The noon of night.

MILKSOP.

n. A soft, mild effeminate, feeble-minded man.

MILLION.

n. A proverbial name for any great number.

MINGLER.

n. He who mingles.

MINUTE-WATCH.

n. A watch in which minutes are more distinctly marked than in common watches which reckon only by the hour.

MISPENDER.

n. One who spends ill or prodigally.

MISPOINT.

v. To confuse sentences by wrong punctuation.

MISS.

n. A term of honour for a young girl.
and
n. A strumpet; a concubine; a whore; a prostitute.

MISTION.

    n. The state of being mingled.

MITTIMUS.

    n. A warrant by which a justice commits an offender to prison.

MIZZY.

    n. A bog; a quagmire.

MNEMONICKS.

    n. The act of memory.

MOBBY.

    n. An American drink made of potatoes.

MOBILE.

    n. The populace; the rout; the mob.

MOHOCK.

    n. The name of a cruel nation of America given to ruffians who infested, or rather were imagined to infest, the streets of London.

MOLEBAT.

    n. A fish.

Mome.
n. A dull stupid blockhead.

Monsieur.
n. A term of reproach for a Frenchman.

Moonstruck.
adj. Lunatic; affected by the moon.

Mope-eyed.
adj. Blind of one eye.

Mopsey.
n. Puppet made of rags.

Morebose.
n. Preceeding from disease; not healthy.

Morling.
n. Wool plucked from a dead sheep.

Mountebank.
n. A doctor that mounts a bench in the market and boasts his infallible remedies and cures.

Mouth-friend.
n. One who professes friendship without intending it.

Mouth-honour.
  n. Civility outwardly expressed without sincerity.

Muchwhat.
  adv. Nearly.

Mucid.
  adj. Slimy; musty.

Muckender.
  n. A handkerchief.

Mucronated.
  n. Narrowed to a sharp point.

Mughouse.
  n. An alehouse; a low house of entertainment.

Mulct.
  v. To punish with fine or forfeiture.

Mullgrubs.
  n. Twisting of the guts.

Mulse.
  n. Wine boiled and mingled with honey.

MUMPER.
n. A beggar.

MUMPS.
n. Sullenness; silent anger.

MUNDIVAGANT.
adj. Wandering through the world.

MUNDUNGUS.
n. Stinking tobacco.

MURAGE.
n. Money paid to keep walls in repair.

MURRAIN.
n. The plague in cattle.

MUTTONFIST.
n. A hand large and red.

MYNCHEN.
n. A nun.

N

NAFF.
   n. A kind of tufted sea-bird.

NAKEDNESS.
   n. Want of provision for defence.

NAPPINESS.
   n. The quality of having a nap.

NARCOTICK.
   adj. Producing torpor or stupefication.

NATATION.
   n. The act of swimming.

NEAF.
   n. A fist. It is retained in Scotland.

Neat.

n. Black cattle, oxen.

Neckbeef.

n. The coarse flesh of the neck of cattle, sold to the poor at a very cheap rate.

Necromancer.

n. One who, by charms, can converse with the ghosts of the dead; a conjurer.

Nectarine.

adj. Sweet as nectar.

Neese.

v. To sneeze; to discharge flatulencies by the nose. Retained in Scotland.

Nepenthe.

n. A drug that drives away all pains.

Nepotism.

n. Fondness of nephews.

Nestegg.

n. An egg left in the nest to keep the hen from forsaking it.

NETTLE.
v. To sting, to irritate.

NEWFANGLED.
adj. Formed with vain or foolish love of novelty.

NICTATE.
v. To wink.

NIDGET.
n. The opprobrious term with which the man was anciently branded who refused to come to the royal standard in times of exigency. A coward; a dastard.

NIDIFICATION.
n. The act of building nests.

NIGHTBRAWLER.
n. One who raises disturbances in the night.

NIGHTDOG.
n. A dog that hunts in the night. Used by deer stealers.

NIM.
v. To take. To steal.

NIMIETY.
    n. The state of being too much.

NINCOMPOOP.
    n. A fool; a trifler.

NINNYHAMMER.
    n. A simpleton.

NIPPINGLY.
    adv. With bitter sarcasm.

NITHING.
    n. A coward; dastard; poltroon.

NITTY.
    adj. Abounding with the eggs of lice.

NIZY.
    n. A dunce; a simpleton.

NOBLESS.
    n. Noblemen collectively.

NOCTAMBULO.
    n. One who walks in his sleep.

NOCTIVAGANT.
   adj. Wandering in the night.

NODATION.
   n. The state of being knotted.

NODDY.
   n. A simpleton; an idiot.

NOMBLES.
   n. The entrails of a deer.

NONAGE.
   n. Minority; time of life before legal maturity.

NONJURING.
   n. One who conceiving James II unjustly deposed, refuses to swear allegiance to those who have succeeded him.

NOODLE.
   n. A fool; a simpleton.

NOONING.
   n. Repose at noon.

NOVERCAL.
    adj. Having the manner of a stepmother.

NOWES.
    n. The marriage knot. Out of use.

NUBBLE.
    v. To bruise with handy cuffs.

NULLIBIETY.
    n. The state of being nowhere.

NUMSKULL.
    n. A dullard; a dunce; a dolt; a blockhead.

NUNCHION.
    n. A piece of victuals eaten between meals.

Oaf.

n. A changeling; a foolish child left by the fairies.

Oats.

n. A grain which in England is generally given to horses but in Scotland supports the people.

Obambulation.

n. The act of walking about.

Obequitation.

n. The act of riding about.

Oberration.

n. The act of wandering about.

Obese.
adj. Fat; loaden with flesh.

Obreption.
n. The act of creeping on.

Obstupefaction.
n. The act of inducing stupidity.

Occlusion.
n. The act of shutting up.

Octonocular.
adj. Having eight eyes.

Odontalgick.
adj. Pertaining to the tooth-ache.

Oeconomicks.
n. Management of household affairs.

Off.
interj. An expression of abhorrence, or command to depart.

Ogle.

v. To view with side glances, as in fondness; or with a design not to be heeded.

Oilman.

n. One who trades in oils and pickles.

Olitory.

n. Belonging to the kitchen garden.

Oneirocritical.

adj. Interpretative of dreams.

Ophiophagous.

adj. Serpent eating.

Opiate.

n. A medicine that causes sleep.

Optimity.

n. The state of being best.

Orniscopist.

n. One who examines the flight of birds in order to foretell futurity.

Oscitation.
n. The act of yawning.

Ospray.
n. The sea eagle, of which it is reported, that when he hovers in the air, all the fish in the water turn up their bellies, and lie still for him to seize which he pleases.

Ouphen.
n. Elfish.

Outknave.
v. To surpass in knavery.

Out-villain.
v. To exceed in villainy.

Ovation.
n. A lesser triumph among the Romans allowed to those commanders who had won a victory without much blood shed, or defeated some less formidable enemy.

Overmuchness.
n. Exhuberance, superabundance.

OVERYEARED.

adj. Too old.

OWLER.

n. One who carries contraband goods illicitly by night.

OXGANG.

n. Twenty acres of land.

OYSTERWENCH.

n. A woman whose business is to sell oysters. A low woman.

P

PADDER.
   n. A robber; a foot highwayman.

PAIGLES.
   n. Cowslips.

PAILMAIL.
   n. Violent; boisterous.

PALACIOUS.
   adj. Royal; noble; magnificent.

PALLET.
   n. A small bed, a mean bed.

PALLIARDISE.
   n. Fornication; whoring.

PALLMALL.
   n. A play in which the ball is struck with a mallet through an iron ring.

PALMER.
   n. A pilgrim; they who returned from the holy land carried branches of palm.

PALMISTRY.
   n. The cheat of foretelling fortune by the lines of the palm.

PAM.
   n. The knave of clubs.

PAMPHLETEER.
   n. A scribbler of small books.

PARAPHERNALIA.
   n. Goods in the wife's disposal.

PARASITE.
   n. One that frequents rich tables and earns his welcome by flattery.

PARBREAK.
   v. To vomit.

Paris.
n. A herb.

Parker.
n. A park keeper.

Parnel.
n. A punk; a slut.

Parricide.
n. One who destroys his father.

Party-jury.
n. A jury in some trials half foreigners and half natives.

Pash.
n. A kiss.

Passion.
n. Violent commotion of the mind.

Passport.
n. Permission of egress.

Patchery.
n. Botchery, bungling work, forgery.

Pathetically.

adv. In such a manner as may strike the passions.

Patibulary.

adj. Belonging to the gallows.

Peace.

n. Respite from war.

Pearleyed.

adj. Having a speck in the eye.

Pedal.

adj. Belonging to the foot.

Pedant.

n. A schoolmaster.

Pedantry.

n. Awkward ostentation of needless learning.

Pedestrious.

adj. Not winged; going on foot.

Peeper.

n. Young chickens just breaking the shell.

Pencil.

n. A small brush of hair which painters dip in their colours.

and

v. To paint.

Penknife.

n. A knife used to cut pens.

Pension.

n. An allowance made to anyone without an equivalent. In England it is generally understood to mean pay given to a state hireling for treason to his country.

Penthouse.

n. A shed hanging out aslope from the main wall.

People.

n. The vulgar.

Pepasticks.

n. Medicines which are good to help the rawness of the stomach and digest crudities.

Peppercorn.

n. Anything of inconsiderable value.

Peppermint.

n. Mint eminently hot.

Periapt.

n. Amulet; charm worn as preservatives against diseases or mischief.

Periergy.

n. Needless caution in an operation; unnecessary diligence.

Periwig.

n. Hair not natural, worn by way of ornament or concealment of baldness.

Permixtion.

n. The act of mingling; the state of being mingled.

Perpender.

n. A coping stone.

Perpotation.

n. The act of drinking largely.

Perspicuity.

n. Clearness to the mind; easiness to be understood; freedom from obscurity or ambiguity.

PERTURBATOUR.
n. Raiser of commotions.

PERUKEMAKER.
n. A wig maker.

PESSARY.
n. An oblong form of medicine, made to thrust up into the uterus upon some extraordinary occasions.

PESTEL.
n. A gammon of bacon.

PESTHOUSE.
n. An hospital for persons infected with the plague.

PETECHIAL.
adj. Pestilentially spotted.

PETROL.
n. A liquid bitumen, black, floating on the water of springs.

PETTIFOGGER.
n. A petty small-rate lawyer.

PETTITOES.
  n. The feet of a sucking pig.

PHASELS.
  n. French beans.

PHILIPPICK.
  adj. Any invective declamation.

PHILOLOGER.
  n. One whose chief study is language.

PHIZ.
  n. The face, in a sense of contempt.

PHYSIOGNOMY.
  n. The act of discovering the temper, and foreknowing the fortune by the features of the face.

PICAROON.
  n. A robber; a plunderer.

PICKEREL-WEED.
  n. A water plant, from which pikes are fabled to be generated.

PICKLE.

n. An small parcel of land enclosed with a hedge, which in some countries is called a pringle.

PICKTHANK.

n. An officious fellow, who does what he is not desired; a whispering parasite.

PICT.

n. A painted person.

PIDDLE.

v. To pick at table; to feed squeamishly and without appetite.

PIGMY.

v. A small nation, fabled to be devoured by the cranes; thence anything mean or inconsiderable.

PIGSNEY.

n. A word of endearment to a girl.

PILOSITY.

n. Hairiness.

PILSER.

n. The moth or fly that runs into a candle flame.

PINK.
v. To wink with the eyes.

PINMONEY.
n. Money allowed to a wife for her private expenses without account.

PINNOCK.
n. The tom-tit.

PIQUERER.
n. A robber, a plunderer.

PIRATE.
n. Any robber; particularly a bookseller who seizes the copies of other men.

PISH.
v. To express contempt.

PITAPAT.
n. A flutter; a palpitation.

PITTANCE.
n. An allowance of meat in a monastery.

PLACKET.
n. A petticoat.

PLASH.
n. A small lake of water or puddle.

PLASTICK.
adj. Having the power to give form.

PLEDGET.
n. A small mass of lint.

PLESH.
n. A puddle; a boggy marsh.

PLUMIPEDE.
n. A fowl that has feathers on the foot.

PLUMPER.
n. Something worn in the mouth to swell out the cheeks.

POLITICIAN.
n. A man of artifice; one of deep contrivance.

POLITICKLY.
adv. Artfully, cunningly.

POLTRON.

n. The practice of cowards to cut off their thumbs, that they might not be compelled to serve in war.

PONK.

n. A nocturnal spirit. A hag.

PORRIDGE.

n. Food made by boiling meat in water.

PORWIGGLE.

n. A tadpole or young frog not yet fully shaped.

POSNET.

n. A little bason; a porringer, a skillet.

POSTER.

n. A courier; one that travels hastily.

POSTUREMASTER.

n. One who teaches or practises artificial contortions of the body.

POTATO.

n. An American word. An esculent root.

POTHER.
    v. To make a blustering ineffectual effort.

POTSHERD.
    n. A fragment of a broken pot.

POTTLE.
    n. Liquid measure containing four pints.

POTVALIANT.
    adj. Heated with courage by strong drink.

POY.
    n. A ropedancer's pole.

PRASON.
    n. A leek; also a seaweed as green as a leek.

PRECOCIOUS.
    adj. Ripe before time.

PRESSGANG.
    n. A crew that strolls about the streets to force men into naval service.

PRICKLOUSE.
 n. A word of contempt for a tailor.

PRIESTCRAFT.
 n. Religious frauds; management of wicked priests to gain power.

PRIG.
 n. A pert, conceited, saucy, pragmatical, little fellow.

PRINCOCK.
 n. A coxcomb, a conceited person; a pert young rogue.

PRIVADO.
 n. A secret friend.

PRIVY.
 n. Place of retirement; necessary house.

PROFESSOR.
 n. One who declares himself of any opinion or party.

PROFLIGATE.
 n. An abandoned shameless wretch.

Prolixness.
n. Tediousness.

Promiscuous.
adj. Mingled; confused; undistinguished.

Prostitute.
n. A public strumpet.

Provender.
n. Dry food for brutes; hay and corn.

Prude.
n. A woman over nice and scrupulous and with false affectation.

Pseudology.
n. A falsehood of speech.

Pshaw.
interj. An expression of contempt.

Puberty.
n. The time of life in which the two sexes begin first to be acquainted.

PUBLICAN.

    n. A toll gatherer.

    and

    n. Man that keeps a house of general entertainment.

PUDDER.

    n. A tumult; a turbulent and irregular bustle.

PUNDLE.

    n. A short and fat woman.

PUNITION.

    n. Punishment.

PUNK.

    n. A whore; a common prostitute; a strumpet.

PUNSTER.

    n. A low wit who endeavours at reputation by double meaning.

PUTID.

    adj. Mean; low; worthless.

PUTTOCK.

    n. A buzzard.

Quack.

n. A boastful pretender to arts which he does not understand.

Quadrin.

n. A mite; a small piece of money, in value about a farthing.

Quaff.

n. He who quaffs.
and
v. To drink; to swallow in large draughts; to drink luxuriously.

Quaggy.

adj. Boggy; soft; not solid.

Quail.

v. To languish, to sink into dejection; to lose spirit.

Qualification.

n. That which makes any person or thing fit for anything.

Qualmish.

adj. Seized with sickly languor.

Quartan.

n. The fourth day ague.

Quartercousins.

n. Not of the four first degrees of kindred, that is they are not friends.

Quean.

n. A worthless woman, generally a strumpet.

Quell.

n. Murder, not in use.

QUEME.

    v. To please. An old word.

QUERIST.

    n. An enquirer; an asker of questions.

QUERPO.

    n. A dress close to the body; a waistcoat.

QUESTERMONGER.

    n. Starter of lawsuits or prosecutions.

QUESTUARY.

    adj. Studious of profit.

QUIBBLER.

    n. A punster.

QUICKEN.

    v. To make alive.

QUIDDANY.

    n. Marmalade. A confection of quinces and sugar.

Quob.

v. To move as the embryo does in the womb; to move as the heart does when throbbing.

Quodlibetarian.

n. One who talks or disputes on any subject.

Quotidian.

n. A fever which returns every day.

R

RACK-RENT.
n. Rent raised to the uttermost.

RAILER.
n. One who insults or defames by opprobrious language.

RAKEHEL.
n. A wild, worthless, dissolute, debauched, sorry-fellow.

RAMBOOZE.
n. A drink made of wine, ale, eggs and sugar in the winter time; or of wine, milk, sugar and rosewater in the summer time.

RAMMISH.
  adj. Strong scented.

RAMPALLIAN.
  n. A mean wretch.

RANNY.
  n. The shrewmouse.

RANTIPOLE.
  n. Wild; roving; rakish.

RAPPER.
  n. One who strikes.

RASCALION.
  n. One of the low people.

RATTLEHEADED.
  adj. Giddy; not steady.

RAWHEAD.
  n. The name of a spectre, mentioned to frighten children.

RAZOURABLE.
  adj. Fit to be shaved.

Rebellow.
v. To bellow in return.

Recrudescent.
adj. Growing painful or violent again.

Recubation.
n. The act of lying or leaning.

Redcoat.
n. A name of contempt for a soldier.

Redshank.
n. A contemptuous appellation for some of the people of Scotland.

Refocillation.
n. Restoration of strength by refreshment.

Refuse.
adj. That which remains disregarded when the rest is taken.

Rememberer.
n. One who remembers.

REMERCIE.

v. To thank, obsolete.

REPASTURE.

n. Entertainment.

REPLEVIN.

v. To take back or set at liberty any thing seized upon security given.

REPROBATE.

n. Lost to virtue; lost to grace; abandoned.

REREMOUSE.

n. A bat.

RESPERSION.

n. The act of sprinkling.

RESUPINATION.

n. The act of lying on the back.

RETROGRADATION.

n. The act of going backwards.

REVERY.
n. Loose musing, irregular thought.

REVESTIARY.
n. Place where dresses are reposited.

REVOMIT.
v. To vomit again.

RHABARBARATE.
adj. Impregnated or tinctured with rhubarb.

RHABDOMANCY.
n. Divination by a wand.

RHEUMATISM.
n. A painful distemper supposed to proceed from acrid humours.

RIBALD.
n. A loose, rough, mean, brutal wretch.

RIBROAST.
v. To beat soundly.

RIC.
n. A powerful, rich or valiant man.

RIDGLING.

n. A ram half castrated.

RIGATION.

n. The act of watering.

RIVER-DRAGON.

n. A crocodile.

RIVER-HORSE.

n. Hippopotamus.

RODOMONTADE.

n. An empty noisy bluster or boast; a rant.

ROLLYPOOLY.

n. A sort of game in which, when a ball rolls into a certain place, it wins.

ROMANCER.

n. A liar; a forger of tales.

ROMP.

n. A rude, awkward, boisterous, untaught girl.

RONION.
n. A fat bulky woman.

RORATION.
n. A falling of dew.

ROTGUT.
n. Bad beer.

ROUNDHOUSE.
n. The constable's prison in which disorderly persons, found in the street, are confined.

ROYNE.
v. To gnaw; to bite.

RUBBAGE.
n. Ruins of building, fragments of matter used in building.

RUDERARY.
adj. Belonging to rubbish.

RUGOSE.
adj. Full of wrinkles.

Rum.

   n. A country parson.

Runnion.

   n. A paltry scurvy wretch.

Rusticate.

   v. To reside in the country.

Rustick.

   n. A clown; a swain; an inhabitant of the country.

S

SABBATHBREAKER.
   n. Violator of the Sabbath by labour or wickedness.

SACRIFICABLE.
   adj. Capable of being offered in sacrifice.

SALAMANDER.
   n. An animal supposed to live in fire and imagined to be very poisonous.

SALAMANDER'S HAIR.
   n. A kind of asbestos or mineral flax.

SALMAGUNDI.
   n. A mixture of chopped meat and pickled herrings with oil, vinegar, pepper and onions.

SALTANT.
    adj. Jumping; dancing.

SALTINBANCO.
    n. A quack or mountebank.

SAMLET.
    n. A little salmon.

SARCOPHAGUS.
    adj. Flesh-eating; feeding on flesh.

SARCULATION.
    n. The act of weeding; plucking up weeds.

SARN.
    n. A British word for pavement or stepping stones, still used in Berkshire and Hampshire.

SASHOON.
    n. A kind of leather stuffing put into a boot for the weaver's ease.

SATELLITE.
    n. A small planet revolving round a larger. Four moons move about Jupiter and five about Saturn.

Saturn.

n. The remotest planet of the solar system. Supposed by astrologers to impress melancholy, dullness or severity of temper.

Saucebox.

n. An impertinent or petulant fellow.

Saveall.

n. A small pan inserted into a candlestick to save the ends of candles.

Scallion.

n. A kind of onion.

Scamble.

v. To be turbulent and rapacious; to scramble; to get by struggling with others.

Scambler.

v. A bold intruder upon one's generosity or table.

Scaramouch.

n. A buffoon in motley dress.

Scatches.

n. Stilts to put the feet in to walk in dirty places.

SCELERAT.

n. A villain; a wicked wretch. A word introduced unnecessarily from the French by a Scottish author.

SCHOOLMAN.

n. One versed in the niceties and subtleties of academical disputation.

SCIATICA.

n. The hip gout.

SCIOMACHY.

n. Battle with a shadow.

SCION.

n. A small twig taken from one tree to be engrafted into another.

SCISSIBLE.

adj. Capable of being divided by a sharp edge.

SCOAT.

v. To stop a wheel by putting a stone or piece of wood under it.

Scold.

n. A clamorous, rude, mean, low, foul-mouthed woman.

Scooper.

n. One who scoops.

Scotch hoppers.

n. A play in which boys hop over lines or scotches in the ground.

Scranch.

v. To grind between the teeth. The Scots retain it.

Screechowl.

n. An owl that hoots in the night and whose voice is supposed to betoken danger, misery or death.

Scroyle.

n. A mean fellow; a rascal; a wretch.

Scuddle.

v. To run with a kind of affected haste or precipitation.

SCULLION.

n. The lowest domestic servant that washes the kettles and the dishes in a kitchen.

SEADOG.

n. Perhaps the shark.

SECOND SIGHT.

n. The power of seeing things future, or things distant; supposed inherent in some of the Scottish islanders.

SEDUCER.

n. One who draws aside from the right; a tempter; a corrupter.

SEEKSORROW.

n. One who contrives to give himself vexation.

SELION.

n. A ridge of land.

SEMIOPACOUS.

adj. Half dark.

SENNIGHT.
   n. The space of seven nights and days; a week.

SERAGLIO.
   n. A house of women kept for debauchery.

SERMOCINATION.
   n. The act or practice of making speeches.

SERVING-MAN.
   n. A menial servant.

SERVITUDE.
   n. Slavery; state of a slave.

SEXTARY.
   n. A pint and a half.

SHALLOP.
   n. A small boat.

SHAMBLES.
   n. The place where butchers kill or sell their meat.

SHAPESMITH.
   n. One who undertakes to improve the form of the body.

SHARPER.
n. A tricking fellow; a petty thief; a rascal.

SHATTERBRAINED.
adj. Inattentive; not confident.

SHEEPBITER.
n. A petty thief.

SHIFTER.
n. One who plays tricks; a man of artifice.

SHILLING.
n. A coin of various value in different times. It is now twelve pence.

SHITTLECOCK.
n. A cork stuck with feathers and driven by players from one to another with battledoors.

SHOEING-HORN.
n. A horn used to facilitate the admission of the foot into a narrow shoe.

SHOG.
n. Violent concussion.

SHOPMAN.
n. A petty trader.

SHORTWAISTED.
adj. Having a short body.

SHOTFREE.
adj. Clear of the reckoning.

SHOULDERSHOTTEN.
adj. Strained in the shoulder.

SHOULDERSLIP.
n. Dislocation of the shoulder.

SHREWMOUSE.
n. A mouse of which the bite is generally supposed venomous, and to which vulgar tradition assigns such malignity, that she is said to lame the foot over which she runs. I am informed that all these reports are calumnious, and that her feet and teeth are equally harmless with those of any other little mouse. Our ancestors however looked on her name with such terror that they are supposed to have given her name to a scolding woman, whom for her venom they call a shrew.

SHRIMP.
n. A little wrinkled man; a dwarf.

SIDEBOX.
n. Seat for the ladies on the side of the theatre.

SIMONY.
n. The crime of buying or selling church preferment.

SINEWSHRUNK.
adj. A horse that has been overridden.

SINGULT.
n. A sigh.

SIXPENCE.
n. A coin; half a shilling.

SKELLUM.
n. A villain; a scoundrel.

SKIMBLESKAMBLE.
adj. Wandering; wild.

SKINKER.
n. One that serves drink.

Skipjack.

n. An upstart.

Skipkennel.

n. A lackey; a footboy.

Slabber.

v. To let spittle fall from the mouth; to drivel.

Slatch.

n. The middle part of a rope or cable that hangs down loose.

Slattern.

n. A woman negligent, not elegant or nice.

Slidder.

v. To slide with interruption.

Slipslop.

n. Bad liquor.

Sloats.

n. Of a cart, are those underpieces which keep the bottom together.

SLUBBERDEGULLION.

n. A paltry, dirty, sorry wretch.

SLUGGARD.

n. An idler; a drone; an inactive lazy fellow.

SLUTISH.

adj. Nasty; not nice; not cleanly; dirty; indecently negligent of cleanliness.

SLUTTERY.

n. The qualities or practice of a slut.

SMATTERER.

n. One who has a slight or superficial knowledge.

SMELLFEAST.

n. A parasite; one who haunts good tables.

SMICKET.

n. The undergarment of a woman.

SNIPSNAP.

n. Tart dialogue.

Solidungulous.
adj. Wholehoofed.

Somerset.
n. A leap by which a jumper throws himself from a beam, and turns over his head.

Sonnetteer.
n. A small poet, in contempt.

Sorcerer.
n. A conjurer; an enchanter; magician.

Soss.
v. To fit lazily on a chair; to fall at once into a chair.

Sot.
v. To tipple to stupidity.

Spaddle.
n. A little spade.

Spanker.
n. A small coin.

Spatterdashes.
n. Coverings for the legs by which the wet is kept off.

Spindleshanked.
adj. Having small legs.

Spitchcock.
v. To cut an eel in pieces and roast him.

Sponk.
n. A word in Edinburgh which denotes a match, or anything dipped in sulphur that takes fire.

Sprit.
v. To throw out; to eject with force.

Sprucebeer.
n. Beer tinctured with branches of fir.

Spruceness.
n. Neatness without elegance.

Spunginghouse.
n. A house to which debtors are taken before commitment to prison where the bailiffs sponge upon them.

SPUTATION.
n. The act of spitting.

SPYBOAT.
n. A boat sent out for intelligence.

SQUALLER.
n. Screamer; one that screams.

SQUIB.
n. Any petty fellow.

SQUINTIFEGO.
adj. Squinting.

STATESMAN.
n. A politician; one versed in the arts of government.

STATESWOMAN.
n. A woman who meddles with public affairs.

STERNUTATION.
n. The act of sneezing.

STEVEN.
n. A cry, or loud clamour.

STEW.

    n. A brothel; a house of prostitution.

STICKLE.

    v. To contest; to altercate; to contend rather with obstinacy than vehemence.

STICKLEBAG.

    n. The smallest of fresh water fish.

STILETTO.

    n. A small dagger, of which the blade is not edged but round, with a sharp point.

STINGO.

    n. Old beer.

STINKARD.

    n. A mean stinking paltry fellow.

STIRIOUS.

    adj. Resembling icicles.

STOAT.

n. A small stinking animal.

STOCKJOBBER.

n. A low wretch who gets money by buying and selling shares in the funds.

STONEHORSE.

n. A horse not castrated.

STOUND.

v. To be in pain or sorrow.

STOUT.

n. Strong; lusty; valiant; brave; bold; intrepid; obstinate; pertinacious; resolute; proud; strong; firm.
and
n. Strong beer.

STRAPPADO.

n. Chastisement by blows.

STRONGWATER.

n. Distilled spirits.

STRUT.
n. An affectation of stateliness in the walk.

STULTILOQUENCE.
n. Foolish talk.

STUM.
n. Wine yet unfermented.

STUPRATE.
v. To ravish; to violate.

STY.
n. Any place of bestial debauchery.

SUBDERISORIOUS.
adj. Scoffing or ridiculing with tenderness and delicacy.

SUBLAPSARY.
adj. Done after the fall of man.

SUBMARINE.
adj. Lying or acting under the sea. These contrivances may seem difficult because submarine navigators will want winds and tides for motion, and the sight of the heavens for direction.

SUCCUMB.
v. To yield; to sink under any difficulty. Not in use, except among the Scotch.

SUDATION.
n. Sweat.

SUDORIFICK.
n. A medicine promoting sweat.

SUGGILATE.
v. To beat black and blue; to make livid by a bruise.

SUICIDE.
n. Self-murder; the horrid crime of destroying one's self.

SUN.
n. The luminary that makes the day.

SUPERVACANEOUSNESS.
n. Needlessness.

SUPPLERLESS.
adj. Wanting supper.

SWAGGERER.

   n. A blusterer; a bully; a turbulent noisy fellow.

SWAIN.

   n. A pastoral youth.

SWALLOW.

   n. A small bird of passage or, as some say, a bird that lies hid and sleeps in winter.

SWANSKIN.

   n. A kind of soft flannel, imitating for warmth the down of a swan.

SWEEPSTAKE.

   n. A man that wins all.

SWILLER.

   n. A luxurious drinker.

SWINEBREAD.

   n. A kind of plant; truffles.

SWINGEBUCKLER.

   n. A bully; a man who pretends to feats of arms.

Swink.

    v. To overlabour.

Swoon.

    v. To suffer a suspension of thought and sensation.

T

TALEBEARER.
    n. One who gives officious or malignant intelligence.

TANTLING.
    n. One seized with hopes of pleasure unobtainable.

TAPSTER.
    n. One whose business is to draw beer in an alehouse.

TARANTULA.
    n. An insect whose bite is only cured by music.

TATTERDEMALION.
    n. A ragged fellow.

Tattle.
v. To talk idly, to use many words with little meaning.

Tattoo.
n. The beat of a drum by which soldiers are warned to their quarters.

Tea.
n. A Chinese plant of which the infusion has lately been much drunk in Europe.

Teague.
n. A name of contempt used for an Irishman.

Ted.
v. To lay grass newly mown in rows.

Teen.
n. Sorrow; grief.

Temulent.
adj. Inebriated; intoxicated as with strong liquors.

Tenebricose.
adj. Dark; gloomy.

TERCE.

n. A vessel containing forty-two gallons of wine; the third part of a butt or pipe.

TERMAGANT.

n. A scold; a brawling turbulent woman.

TESTUDINEOUS.

adj. Resembling the shell of a tortoise.

THESMOTHETE.

n. A lawgiver.

THICKSKIN.

n. A coarse, gross man; a numskull.

THORAL.

adj. Relating to the bed.

THRAPPLE.

n. The windpipe of any animal. They still retain it in the Scottish dialect.

THRASONICAL.

adj. Boastful; bragging.

Threepenny.
adj. Vulgar; mean.

Threepile.
n. An old name for good velvet.

Thrid.
n. To slide through a narrow passage.

Thryfallow.
v. To give the third ploughing in summer.

Tiddle.
v. To use tenderly; to fondle.

Tillyfally.
adj. Anything said rejected as trifling or impertinent.

Tipple.
v. To drink luxuriously; to waste life over the cup.

Tirewoman.
n. A woman whose business is to make dresses for the head.

Tit.
n. A woman; in contempt.

Titubation.
n. The act of stumbling.

Toad.
n. An animal resembling a frog; but the frog leaps, the toad crawls; the toad is accounted venomous, I believe truly.

Toilet.
n. A dressing table.

Tolutation.
n. The act of pacing or ambling.

Tomboy.
n. A mean course fellow; sometimes a wild course girl.

Tonguepad.
n. A great talker.

Toot.
v. To pry; to peep; to search narrowly and slily.

Toothdrawer.

n. One whose business is to extract painful teeth.

Topsyturvy.

adv. With bottom upward.

Torpedo.

n. A fish which while alive, if touched even with a long stick benumbs the hand that so touches it, but when dead is eaten safely.

Torrefaction.

n. The act of drying by the fire.

Tosspot.

n. A toper and drunkard.

Tranters.

n. Men who carry fish from the sea coast to sell in the inland countries.

Trape.

v. To run idly and sluttishly about. It is used only of women.

TRAVELTAINTED.
   adj. Harassed; fatigued by travel.

TRAVESTY.
   adj. Dressed so as to be made ridiculous; burlesqued.

TREMENDOUS.
   adj Dreadful; horrible; astonishingly terrible.

TRENCHERMATE.
   n. A table companion; a parasite.

TRICKSY.
   adj. Pretty. A word of endearment.

TRIPUDATION.
   n. The act of dancing.

TROCHILICKS.
   n. The science of rotary motion.

TROLLOP.
   n. A slatternly, loose woman.

TROT.
   n. An old woman. In contempt.

Troy-weight.
n. A kind of weight by which gold and bread are weighed, consisting of these denominations: a pound = 12 ounces; ounce = 20 pennyweights; pennyweight = 24 grains.

Trubtail.
n. A short squat woman.

Trucidation.
n. The act of killing.

Truepenny.
n. A familiar phrase for an honest fellow.

Trull.
n. A low whore; a vagrant strumpet.

Tush.
interj. An expression of contempt.

Tuz.
n. A lock or tuft of hair.

Twangling.
adj. Contemptibly noisy.

Twibil.

    n. A halbert.

Twittletwattle.

    n. Tattle; gabble.

Tympany.

    n. A kind of obstructed flatulence that swells the body like a drum.

Tyrannicide.

    n. The act of killing a tyrant.

Umpire.

   n. A common friend who decides disputes.

Unbid.

   adj. Uninvited.

Underfellow.

   n. A mean man; a sorry wretch.

Understrapper.

   n. A petty fellow; an inferior agent.

Unicorn.

   n. A beast, whether real or fabulous, that has only one horn.

UNIVERSE.
  n. The general system of things.

UNPREGNANT.
  adj. Not prolific.

UNRAZORED.
  adj. Unshaven.

UNWHIPT.
  adj. Not punished; not corrected with the rod.

URCHIN.
  n. A hedge-hog.

URINAL.
  n. A bottle in which water is kept for inspection.

URINATOR.
  n. A diver; one who searches under water.

USQUEBAUGH.
  n. The water of life. A compounded, distilled, aromatic spirit; the Irish sort is particularly distinguished for its pleasant and mild flavour. The Highland sort is somewhat hotter; in Scottish they call it whisky.

USTION.
n. The act of burning; the state of being burned.

USTORIOUS.
adj. Having the quality of burning.

UXORIOUS.
adj. Submissively fond of a wife; infected with connubial dotage.

VACATION.
n. Leisure; freedom from trouble or perplexity.

VACCARY.
n. A cow house; a cow-pasture.

VALLANCY.
n. A large wig that shades the face.

VANCOURIER.
n. A harbinger.

VAPORER.
n. A boaster; a braggart.

VARLET.

n. A scoundrel; a rascal.

VARVELS.

n. Silver rings about the leg of a hawk, in which the owner's name is engraved.

VASTATION.

n. Waste; depopulation.

VATICIDE.

n. A murderer of poets.

VAUDEVIL.

n. A song common among the vulgar, and sung about the streets.

VAUNTER.

n. Boaster; braggart; man given to vain ostentation.

VENEFICE.

n. The practice of poisoning.

VENERY.

n. The sport of hunting.

VERECUND.
   n. Modest; bashful.

VESPERTINE.
   adj. Happening or coming in the evening; pertaining to the evening.

VEST.
   n. An outer garment.

VIDUITY.
   n. Widowhood.

VIGESIMATION.
   n. The act of putting to death every twentieth man.

VINNEWED.
   adj. Mouldy.

VIRAGO.
   n. A female warrior; a woman with the qualities of a man.

VIRGINITY.
   n. Maidenhead.

Vitious.

adj. Corrupt; wicked; opposite to virtuous. It is applied rather to habitual faults, than criminal actions.

Viz.

n. To wit; that is. A barbarous form of an unnecessary word.

Volery.

n. A flight of birds.

Voluptuary.

n. A man given up to pleasure and luxury.

Vulgar.

v. The common people.

Vulpine.

adj. Belonging to the fox.

WAG.

  n. Anyone ludicrously mischievous; a merry droll.

WAGGLE.

  v. To waddle; to move from side to side.

WAID.

  adj. Crushed.

WAIR.

  n. A piece of timber two yards long and a foot broad.

WALLOP.

  v. To boil.

WAMBLE.
v. To roll with nausea and sickness. It is used of the stomach.

WANTWIT.
v. A fool; an idiot.

WAPED.
adj. Dejected; crushed by misery.

WARDROBE.
n. A room where clothes are kept.

WARLING.
n. One often quarrelled with.

WARLOCK.
n. A male witch; a wizard. In Scotland it is applied to a man whom the vulgar suppose to be conversant with the spirits, as a woman who carries on the same commerce is called a witch.

WARMINGSTONE.
n. Useful stones digged in Cornwall, which being once heated at the fire retains its warmth a great while, and hath been found to give ease in the internal haemorrhoids.

WARRAY.

v. To make war upon.

WARWORN.

adj. Worn with war.

WASSAIL.

n. A liquor made of apples, sugar and ale, anciently much used by English goodfellows.

WATCHET.

adj. Pale blue.

WATERMELON.

n. A plant. It hath trailing branches as the cucumber or melon and is distinguished from other cucurbitaceous plants by its leaf deeply cut and jagged and by its producing uneatable fruit.

WAWL.

v. To cry; to howl.

WEATHERSPY.

n. A star-gazer; an astrologer; one that foretells the weather.

WEED.
　　n. A herb noxious or useless.

WEEKDAY.
　　n. Any day not Sunday.

WEEN.
　　v. To think, to imagine, to form a notion, to fancy.

WELAWAY.
　　interj. Alas.

WELLWILLER.
　　n. One who means kindly.

WENCHER.
　　n. A fornicator.

WHERRET.
　　v. To give a box on the ear.

WHIFFLE.
　　v. To move inconstantly, as if driven by a puff of wind.

WHIMPLED.
　　adj. Distorted with crying.

Whipster.
  n. A nimble fellow.

Whoobub.
  n. Hubbub.

Whore.
  v. To converse unlawfully with the other sex.

Whurr.
  v. To pronounce the letter r with too much force.

Widowhunter.
  n. One who courts widows for a jointure.

Widowmaker.
  n. One who deprives women of their husbands.

Wife.
  n. A woman of low employment.

Wight.
  adj. Swift; nimble.

Wildgoosechase.
  n. A pursuit of something as unlikely to be caught as the wild goose.

WILLI.
adj. Many.

WIMBLE.
adj. Active; nimble; shifting to and fro.

WHIMPLE.
n. A hood; a veil.

WINDEGG.
n. An egg not impregnated; an egg that does not contain the principles of life.

WINTERBEATEN.
adj. Harassed by severe weather.

WISEACRE.
n. A wise, or sententious man.
and
n. A fool; a dunce.

WITLING.
n. A pretender to wit; a man of petty smartness.

WITTOL.
n. A man who knows the falsehood of his wife and seems contented; a tame cuckhold.

WITWORM.

   n. One that feeds on wit; a canker of wit.

WOEBEGONE.

   n. Lost in woe; distracted in woe, overwhelmed in sorrow.

WOODNOTE.

   n. Wild music.

WORKHOUSE.

   n. A place where idlers and vagabonds are condemned to labour.

WORKYDAY.

   n. A day not the Sabbath.

WOT.

   v. To know; to be aware.

WRETCH.

   n. A miserable mortal. A worthless sorry creature.

X is a letter, which though found in Saxon, begins
no word in the English language.

YARR.
    v. To growl, or snarl like a dog.

YELK.
    n. The yellow part of the egg. Often written yolk.

YESTERNIGHT.
    n. The night before this night.

YOND.
    adj. Mad, furious.

YUCK.
    n. Itch.

YUX.
    n. The hiccough.

Z

ZANY.

n. One employed to raise laughter by his gestures, actions and speeches; a merry-andrew; a buffoon.

ZEPHYR.

n. The west wind and, poetically, any calm soft wind.

ZOOTOMIST.

n. A dissector of the bodies of brute beasts.